LeBron JAMES

VS.

Michael JORDAN

By Brian Howell

SportsZone

An Imprint of Abdo Publishing
abdopublishing.com

abdopublishing.com

Published by Abdo Publishing, a division of ABDO, PO Box 398166, Minneapolis, Minnesota 55439. Copyright © 2018 by Abdo Consulting Group, Inc. International copyrights reserved in all countries. No part of this book may be reproduced in any form without written permission from the publisher. SportsZone™ is a trademark and logo of Abdo Publishing.

Printed in the United States of America, North Mankato, Minnesota
102017
072018

Distributed in paperback by North Star Editions, Inc.

Cover Photos: Wilfredo Lee/AP Images, left; Tom DiPace/AP Images, right
Interior Photos: Tom DiPace/AP Images, 4–5; Tony Dejak/AP Images, 5; Bruce Bennett/ Getty Images, 6–7; David Richard/AP Images, 8; Ronald Martinez/AP Images, 10–11; Ron Frehm/AP Images, 13; Ross D. Franklin/AP Images, 14–15; Fred Jewell/AP Images, 17; Alan Diaz/AP Images, 18–19; Roberto Borea/AP Images, 20; Eric Risberg/AP Images, 22; Ron Schwane/AP Images, 24–25; Nick Ut/AP Images, 26; Gene J. Puskar/AP Images, 27; Michael Conroy/AP Images, 29

Editor: Patrick Donnelly
Series Designer: Sarah Winkler

Publisher's Cataloging-in-Publication Data
Names: Howell, Brian, author.
Title: LeBron James vs. Michael Jordan / by Brian Howell.
Other titles: LeBron James versus Michael Jordan
Description: Minneapolis, Minnesota : Abdo Publishing, 2018. | Series: Versus | Includes
     online resources and index.
Identifiers: LCCN 2017946927 | ISBN 9781532113550 (lib.bdg.) |
     ISBN: 9781641852999 (pbk) | ISBN 9781532152436 (ebook)
Subjects: LCSH: Basketball players--Juvenile literature. | Basketball--Records--United
     States--Juvenile literature. | Sports--History--Juvenile literature.
Classification: DDC 796.323--dc23
LC record available at https://lccn.loc.gov/2017946927

TABLE OF CONTENTS

INTRODUCTION

Basketball is a team sport, but one-on-one matchups take place all over the court. Fans can usually tell who outplayed the opponent on any given night. But how do you compare players from different eras?

Michael Jordan is widely considered the best to ever play in the National Basketball Association (NBA). With six championship rings, ten scoring titles, and five Most Valuable Player (MVP) Awards, it's hard to disagree. Until you consider LeBron James, that is. He's got three rings and four MVP trophies, and he was still going strong in 2017.

Which one was better? It's an argument without a right or wrong answer. We'll tell their stories and lay out the facts.

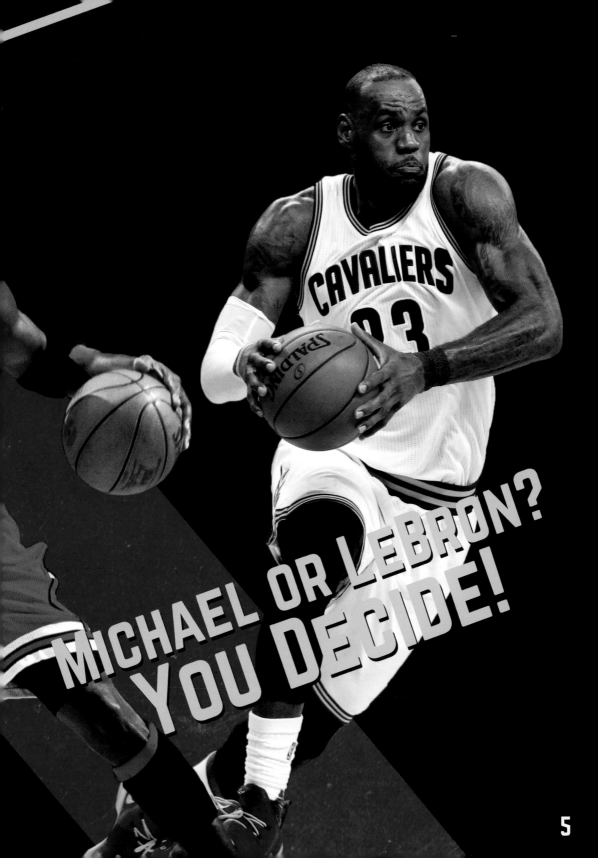

MICHAEL OR LEBRON? YOU DECIDE!

Michael Jordan's agility and body control came in handy when he took the ball to the basket.

CHAPTER 1

SCORING

Michael Jordan launched himself into the air. With his tongue hanging out and the ball in his right hand, the Chicago Bulls superstar flew toward the basket. Everybody watching the game expected Jordan to deliver another amazing dunk.

But, while in midair, Jordan noticed a defender in his way. At the last moment, Jordan moved the ball to his left hand. On his way down, he flipped the ball off the backboard and through the hoop. It was another spectacular basket for Jordan, a man known for making the amazing look routine. It was just one of many great moments in the 1991 NBA Finals, when Jordan and the Bulls defeated the Los Angeles Lakers.

Nearly 20 years later, LeBron James and the Cleveland Cavaliers trailed the Orlando Magic by two points with only one second left in an important playoff game. A teammate threw the ball inbounds to James. He caught it, soared above his defender, and launched a long shot.

LeBron James launches a buzzer-beating three-pointer to defeat the Orlando Magic in the 2009 NBA playoffs.

As the buzzer sounded, the ball dropped through the hoop for a three-pointer and a Cavaliers victory.

Throughout the history of basketball there have been a lot of great scorers. Jordan and James are two of the most talented scorers to ever play.

There's a lot more to being a great scorer than simply piling up points. The great ones know how to score in many ways. The best can score in creative ways, as Jordan did against the Lakers. They also score in dramatic ways, as James did against the Magic.

Comparing only their scoring averages, it would be easy to give the advantage to Jordan. During his 15-year career, Jordan averaged an amazing 30.1 points per game. That's an NBA record. He also won a record 10 scoring titles. No other player has won more than seven. Meanwhile, through 2017 James had played 14 seasons, averaging 27.1 points per game.

One other factor to consider is that James's totals all come from the prime of his career. Jordan sat out almost two full seasons at age 30 and 31—still peak scoring years—when he temporarily retired after leading the Bulls to three straight NBA titles. His stats also include a sharp decline in his final two seasons when he came out of retirement again at age 38 to play for the Washington Wizards. Subtract those two seasons from his totals and his career average jumps to an incredible 31.5 points per game.

But points alone don't tell the story of these two great players. While James has scored fewer points, he has also taken fewer shots than Jordan. In fact, Jordan averaged about three more shot attempts per game than James has averaged.

James has actually been a slightly better shooter than Jordan was. James made 50.1 percent of his shots through his first 14 seasons, including 34.2 percent from three-point range.

CAVS.COM.   .#NBAFinals

James uses his size and strength to get position inside, where he puts back his teammates' missed shots for easy baskets.

Jordan made 49.7 percent of his career shots, including 32.7 percent from beyond the arc.

There's one area in which Jordan has a big advantage over James—at the free-throw line. Jordan was deadly from the line, shooting 83.5 percent over the course of his career. James has been good, but not great, checking in at 74.0 percent.

During their careers, Jordan and James both displayed the ability to score from anywhere on the court. They came through in some of their teams' most crucial moments. They both delivered many last-second, game-winning shots. But they were different types of scorers.

The style of play in the NBA has changed a bit since Jordan retired. Teams are emphasizing the three-pointer much more than in the past. So it makes sense that James has relied much more on three-pointers. Through 2017 he had already taken more than twice as many three-point shots as Jordan did in his entire career.

James also became a more accurate shooter as his career went along. In his first eight seasons, he made 32.9 percent of his three-pointers. He bumped that average up to 36.1 over his next six seasons. His shooting percentage also climbed as he improved his inside game. Using his big body, James learned to put his back to the basket and beat opponents in the low post, resulting in many more attempts closer to the hoop.

Jordan was exceptional at getting to the rim and scoring on dunks and layups. With his talent and creativity, he may have

MEET THE PLAYERS

MICHAEL JORDAN

- Born February 17, 1963, in Brooklyn, New York
- 6 feet, 6 inches/195 pounds
- Attended the University of North Carolina, 1981–84
- Home today: Charlotte, North Carolina

LEBRON JAMES

- Born December 30, 1984, in Akron, Ohio
- 6 feet, 8 inches/250 pounds
- Went straight to the NBA from Saint Vincent-Saint Mary High School in Akron
- Home today: Bath Township, Ohio

been the best player ever around the rim. And Jordan knew how to use those scoring skills to take over games. He poured in 50 or more points in a game 31 times (compared to just 10 times for James). Those outbursts included a career-high 69 points in a 1990 game against Cleveland and a 55-point game against the New York Knicks in 1995, in just his fifth game back after taking a year and a half away from the game in his prime.

Jordan also learned how to change his game as he got older. Specifically, he took—and made—a lot more three-pointers. Jordan had only five seasons with more than 100 three-pointers, but three of those seasons were his last three with the Bulls. He made 36.9 percent of his threes in that stretch.

While they were different types of scorers, neither could be easily stopped. And both worked hard to turn their weaknesses into strengths.

Jordan goes inside to score two of his 55 points against the Knicks in 1995.

James is able to outmuscle most players when battling for a rebound.

CHAPTER 2

REBOUNDING

Jordan was a shooting guard. James has mostly played small forward. Neither position is expected to contribute many rebounds. But both players proved to be excellent rebounders anyway.

Height and talent help players grab rebounds. Perhaps the most important quality to being a great rebounder, however, is the desire to go get the ball. That requires playing hard all the time. Few played harder than James and Jordan. During Game 3 of the 2016 NBA Finals, James showed what extra effort can do. He missed a shot near the basket, but he outmuscled three Golden State Warriors to grab the rebound. Powering past the defenders, he went back to the basket and scored.

At 6 feet, 8 inches tall and 250 pounds, James is a big, powerful man. As the

PROFESSIONAL SUCCESS

MICHAEL JORDAN

- First NBA game: October 26, 1984
- Years active: 1984–93, 1995–98, 2001–03
- NBA titles: 6 in 6 Finals appearances
- All-Star Games: 14

LEBRON JAMES

- First NBA game: October 29, 2003
- Years active: 2003–present
- NBA titles: 3 in 8 Finals appearances through 2017
- All-Star Games: 13 through 2017

Warriors found out during that series, his size and power make him a good rebounder. But he doesn't just rely on his body to collect rebounds. He is a smart player. Because of that, he knows how to get in position to get the rebound. And when the ball bounces off the basket, he stops at nothing to get to it.

Bigger and stronger than Jordan, it's little surprise that James has posted better rebounding numbers. Jordan averaged 6.2 per game in his career, with a peak season average of 8.0. Through his first 14 years, James averaged 7.3 rebounds per game with a career-high season average of 8.6.

But statistics don't tell the whole story. Opportunity is an important factor in comparing rebounding stats, and Jordan played with some great rebounders. When you've got Charles Oakley, Horace Grant, and Dennis Rodman on your side, you don't have the need—or the chance—to grab many rebounds.

But when his team needed it, Jordan knew how to get the ball. He often made his rebounds looks amazing, too.

During one game against the Portland Trail Blazers, Scottie Pippen of the Bulls was shooting a free throw. Jordan waited behind the three-point line. As Pippen released the ball, Jordan exploded toward the basket and launched himself into the air.

Pippen's shot missed, but before anyone else could get into position for the rebound, Jordan grabbed the ball with one hand in midair and slammed it home for a dunk.

That play was possible because, like James, Jordan was a smart player. That allowed him to be in the right position to get many of his rebounds.

Jordan wasn't asked to crash the boards often, but when he did, his athletic ability helped him get to the ball before other players could get a hand on it.

Jordan sticks close to Dan Majerle of the Miami Heat in a 1996 game.

CHAPTER 3

DEFENSE

Trying to stop James and Jordan from scoring proved difficult for everybody in the NBA. Trying to score against James and Jordan wasn't easy, either.

Throughout their careers, both players provided amazing moments on offense. But they also took great pride in their defense.

Jordan loved stopping his opponents. He frustrated many of the game's best players during his career. During a game against the Indiana Pacers, Jordan was guarding star Reggie Miller. One of the best shooters in the NBA, Miller was a thorn in the sides of even the best defenders.

On one play, Miller tried to beat Jordan off the dribble. Jordan never took his eyes off Miller. As Miller tried

Jordan used his quick hands and experience to strip the ball away from his opponents.

to go around him, Jordan slapped at the ball. He knocked the ball out of Miller's hands and stole it. Seconds later Jordan raced down to the other end of the court and scored.

The play showcased Jordan's quickness and tenacity. He was quick enough to guard small, fast point guards. He was also big enough and strong enough to guard bigger players.

With Jordan's combination of quickness and strength, opponents had a hard time getting around him. They also had a hard time passing the ball. Jordan's hands often seemed to be in the way. That caused a lot of bad passes and turnovers.

One of the best defensive plays Jordan ever made came during his last game with the Bulls. The Utah Jazz led the Bulls by one point with 25 seconds to play in Game 6 of the 1998 NBA Finals.

MICHAEL JORDAN

- NBA Finals per-game averages: 33.6 points, 6.0 rebounds, 6.0 assists, 48.1 field goal percentage
- Career highlight: Jordan hit the game-winning shot to beat Utah and clinch his sixth NBA title in 1998.
- Awards: NBA MVP (1988, 1991, 1992, 1996, 1998); NBA Finals MVP (1991, 1992, 1993, 1996, 1997, 1998); NBA Rookie of the Year (1985); NBA All-Star Game MVP (1988, 1996, 1998)
- Record in playoff series: 30–7

LEBRON JAMES

- NBA Finals per-game averages: 27.7 points, 10.1 rebounds, 7.5 assists, 46.7 field goal percentage
- Career highlight: James led the Cavaliers back from a 3-to-1 deficit in the 2016 NBA Finals to win a championship for his home state.
- Awards: NBA MVP (2009, 2010, 2012, 2013); NBA Finals MVP (2012, 2013, 2016); NBA Rookie of the Year (2004); NBA All-Star Game MVP (2006, 2008)
- Record in playoff series: 32–9

Utah's John Stockton passed the ball to power forward Karl Malone. Less than a second later, Jordan came from behind and knocked the ball out of Malone's hands for a steal. Moments later, Jordan hit the game-winning shot to secure his and the Bulls' sixth NBA championship.

Jordan won the NBA's Defensive Player of the Year Award in 1988 and was named to the NBA's All-Defensive First Team nine times, which is an NBA record.

James made one of the biggest defensive plays in the history of the NBA Finals when he blocked Andre Iguodala's shot in 2016.

James has also proven able to defend different types of players. He had enough athletic ability to stop quick guards. With his size and strength, he could also handle big players. And he studied the game closely, which allowed him to understand and predict how his opponents would play.

"I've always taken that side of the floor very seriously, and being able to guard multiple positions, being able to know what teams are doing out on the floor, and putting my teammates in position to be successful . . . that's always been something I've taken pride in," James said.

One of the most memorable plays of his career came on defense. Game 7 of the 2016 NBA Finals was tied with less than two minutes to play. The Golden State Warriors started a fast break. Stephen Curry passed the ball to teammate Andre Iguodala, who appeared to be heading for an easy two points.

But as Iguodala's layup hit the backboard, James came flying into the play. Soaring high, James pinned the ball to the glass, snuffing Iguodala's shot and swinging the momentum to the Cavaliers. They went on to win the game and the NBA championship. It was Cleveland's first championship in any major professional sport since 1964. James's great defensive play helped to make it happen.

While James was never voted defensive player of the year, he is known as a great defender. He was named to the NBA's All-Defensive First Team five times and the second team once.

James often directs traffic when the Cavs have the ball.

CHAPTER 4

LEADERSHIP

Jordan and James have always been known as winners. They also were the leaders of winning teams during their careers.

Jordan was one of the great champions in the history of basketball. As a freshman at the University of North Carolina in 1982, he hit the game-winning shot in the national championship game. In the NBA, it took him a few years to win a title. Once he did, he just kept winning. Jordan led the Chicago Bulls to six NBA titles.

Jordan was the heart of the championship Bulls teams in the 1990s. He helped them win championships in 1991, 1992, and 1993. He retired from the NBA after the 1993 season, and Chicago couldn't win without him.

When Jordan returned, the Bulls started winning again. He led them to championships in 1996, 1997,

Jordan never seemed to mind being the face of the franchise during his NBA career.

and 1998. During his NBA career, Jordan reached the Finals six times and won every time.

This success was no surprise to those who followed the Bulls. Jordan was known for his killer instinct. He badly wanted to win, and he held his teammates accountable. If they weren't working hard enough, he let them know it. As a team leader, Jordan elevated all the players around him.

Jordan wasn't just a great talent. Nobody was better in the clutch than Jordan. Many of his greatest moments were created in the final seconds of big games, such as when he clinched two playoff series with huge shots on the road, against the Cavaliers in 1989 and the Jazz in 1998.

James has not won as much as Jordan, but he still has three NBA championships to his credit. James led the Miami Heat to championships in 2012 and 2013. Then in 2016, he took his hometown Cavaliers to their first NBA title.

While he doesn't have as many championships, James has been to the Finals more than Jordan. Through his first 14 seasons, James took his teams to the Finals eight times, including seven in a row from 2011 to 2017.

James made the Cavaliers better from the moment he arrived as a rookie in the 2003–04 season. Cleveland won just 17 games before he arrived. In his rookie year, James helped the Cavaliers to 35 wins. In his third year, they won 50 games.

James will forever be revered in Cleveland for bringing a championship to his hometown.

MICHAEL JORDAN

- Important records: most points per game, career (30.1); most points per playoff game, career (33.4); most seasons leading league in scoring (10); most consecutive seasons leading league in scoring (7, tied with Wilt Chamberlain)

- Key rivals: Detroit Pistons, New York Knicks

- Off-court accomplishments: owner of NBA's Charlotte Hornets; Make-A-Wish Foundation Chief Wish Ambassador; established James R. Jordan Boys & Girls Club of Chicago and Jordan Institute for Families at University of North Carolina

"You don't hesitate with Michael, or you'll end up on some poster in a gift shop someplace."

—Former NBA center Felton Spencer

LEBRON JAMES

- Important records: most career points scored in the playoffs (6,163); most career points in All-Star Games (291)

- Key rivals: San Antonio Spurs, Golden State Warriors

- Off-court accomplishments: launched LeBron James Family Foundation in 2004; pledged $1 million to his former high school to rebuild the gymnasium; regularly works with Boys & Girls Clubs of America

"He's the Einstein of basketball. . . . What he's done is mind-blowing, with what he's had to work with."

—Basketball Hall of Famer Isiah Thomas

James took Cleveland to the playoffs five years in a row. Then he left for Miami. Without James the Cavaliers were one of the worst teams in the NBA, while James took the Heat to the Finals four years straight. Then in 2014, James went back to Cleveland. Instantly the Cavaliers were one of the best teams in the league again.

Although he is very talented, James works hard and leads by example. He shares his wisdom and helps his teammates improve. As a result, James's teams often improve, too.

Jordan and James were great at scoring. They were great at rebounding. They were great at defense. Above all they were great at winning.

When Jordan was on the floor, there was never any doubt who was in charge.

GLOSSARY

CLUTCH
An important or pressure-packed situation.

DRAMATIC
Striking in appearance or effect.

EMPHASIZE
To place importance on.

FAST BREAK
Moving the ball up the floor quickly.

FRESHMAN
A first-year player.

LAYUP
A shot made from close to the basket; an easy shot.

POST
The area around the basket where power forwards and centers usually play.

REBOUND
To catch the ball after a shot has been missed.

SNUFFING
Ending or extinguishing.

ONLINE RESOURCES

Booklinks
NONFICTION NETWORK
FREE! ONLINE NONFICTION RESOURCES

To learn more about great basketball players, visit abdobooklinks.com. These links are routinely monitored and updated to provide the most current information available.

MORE INFORMATION

BOOKS

De Medeiros, Michael. *The NBA Finals*. New York: Smartbook Media Inc., 2018.

Gitlin, Marty. *LeBron James*. Minneapolis, MN: Abdo Publishing, 2017.

Hawkins, Jeff. *Michael Jordan: Basketball Superstar and Commercial Icon*. Minneapolis, MN: Abdo Publishing, 2014.

INDEX

ABOUT THE AUTHOR

Brian Howell is a freelance writer based in Denver, Colorado. He has been a sports journalist for more than 20 years and has written dozens of books about sports and American history. A native of Colorado, he lives with his wife and four children.